Gift of the
Prestons

SPORTS GREAT JASON KIDD

—Sports Great Books—

BASEBALL

Sports Great Jim Abbott
0-89490-395-0/ Savage

Sports Great Barry Bonds
0-89490-595-3/ Sullivan

Sports Great Bobby Bonilla
0-89490-417-5/ Knapp

Sports Great Orel Hershiser
0-89490-389-6/ Knapp

Sports Great Bo Jackson
0-89490-281-4/ Knapp

Sports Great Greg Maddux
0-89490-873-1/ Thornley

Sports Great Kirby Puckett
0-89490-392-6/ Aaseng

Sports Great Cal Ripken, Jr.
0-89490-387-X/ Macnow

Sports Great Nolan Ryan
0-89490-394-2/ Lace

Sports Great Darryl Strawberry
0-89490-291-1/ Torres & Sullivan

BASKETBALL

Sports Great Charles Barkley
Revised Edition
0-7660-1004-X/ Macnow

Sports Great Larry Bird
0-89490-368-3/ Kavanagh

Sports Great Muggsy Bogues
0-89490-876-6/ Rekela

Sports Great Patrick Ewing
0-89490-369-1/ Kavanagh

Sports Great Anfernee Hardaway
0-89490-758-1/ Rekela

Sports Great Magic Johnson
Revised and Expanded
0-89490-348-9/ Haskins

Sports Great Michael Jordan
Revised Edition
0-89490-978-9/ Aaseng

Sports Great Jason Kidd
0-7660-1001-5/ Torres

Sports Great Karl Malone
0-89490-599-6/ Savage

Sports Great Reggie Miller
0-89490-874-X/ Thornley

Sports Great Alonzo Mourning
0-89490-875-8/ Fortunato

Sports Great Hakeem Olajuwon
0-89490-372-1/ Knapp

Sports Great Shaquille O'Neal
Revised Edition
0-7660-1003-1/ Sullivan

Sports Great Scottie Pippen
0-89490-755-7/ Bjarkman

Sports Great David Robinson
Revised Edition
0-7660-1077-5/ Aaseng

Sports Great Dennis Rodman
0-89490-759-X/ Thornley

Sports Great John Stockton
0-89490-598-8/ Aaseng

Sports Great Isiah Thomas
0-89490-374-8/ Knapp

Sports Great Dominique Wilkins
0-89490-754-9/ Bjarkman

FOOTBALL

Sports Great Troy Aikman
0-89490-593-7/ Macnow

Sports Great Jerome Bettis
0-89490-872-3/Majewski

Sports Great John Elway
0-89490-282-2/ Fox

Sports Great Brett Favre
0-7660-1000-7/ Savage

Sports Great Jim Kelly
0-89490-670-4/ Harrington

Sports Great Joe Montana
0-89490-371-3/ Kavanagh

Sports Great Jerry Rice
0-89490-419-1/ Dickey

Sports Great Barry Sanders
0-89490-418-3/ Knapp

Sports Great Emmitt Smith
0-7660-1002-3/ Grabowski

Sports Great Herschel Walker
0-89490-207-5/ Benagh

HOCKEY

Sports Great Wayne Gretzky
0-89490-757-3/ Rappoport

Sports Great Mario Lemieux
0-89490-596-1/ Knapp

Sports Great Eric Lindros
0-89490-871-5/ Rappoport

TENNIS

Sports Great Steffi Graf
0-89490-597-X/ Knapp

Sports Great Pete Sampras
0-89490-756-5/ Sherrow

SPORTS GREAT
JASON KIDD

John Albert Torres

—Sports Great Books—

Enslow Publishers, Inc.

44 Fadem Road   PO Box 38
Box 699   Aldershot
Springfield, NJ 07081   Hants GU12 6BP
USA   UK

Library of Congress Cataloging-in-Publication Data

Torres, John Albert.
    Sports great Jason Kidd / John Albert Torres.
       p. cm. — (Sports great books)
    Includes index.
    Summary: Profiles the personal life and basketball career of Jason Kidd, the star point guard who left the University of California after his sophomore season.
    ISBN 0-7660-1001-5
    1. Kidd, Jason—Juvenile literature. 2. Basketball players—United States— Biography—Juvenile literature. 3. Dallas Mavericks (Basketball team)—Juvenile literature. [1. Kidd, Jason. 2. Basketball players.] I. Title. II. Series.
    GV884.K53T67 1998
    796.323'092—dc21
    [B]   97-18076
                                                CIP
                                                AC

Printed in the United States of America

10 9 8 7 6 5 4 3 2 1

Illustration Credits: AP/Wide World Photos, p. 59; Bill Kostroun, pp. 9, 10, 13, 15, 19, 23, 26, 28, 32, 36, 38, 41, 44, 47, 49, 53, 55.

Cover Illustration: AP/Wide World Photos.

Contents

Chapter 1

The game was destined to be a classic. The torch was being passed from one great athlete to another. On one side of the court were the defending college basketball champion Duke Blue Devils, led by their great point guard, Bobby Hurley. He had become the NCAA's all-time leader in assists. He also had led his team to the last two national championships.

At the other end of the floor were the underdog California Golden Bears, with new head coach Todd Bozeman and led by freshman point guard and future superstar Jason Kidd.

The Golden Bears had advanced in the tournament and were set to play Duke because of Jason Kidd himself. California was tied with Louisiana State University (LSU) late in the first game of the NCAA tournament. With only five seconds left in the game, Kidd dribbled the basketball into the middle of the Tiger defense. He made a nasty spin move, and split forward Lenear Burns and center Geert Hammink. Then he threw up a shot, high off the backboard, that fell right through the basket. Kidd had won the game. The game-winning shot became known as the "pretzel" shot because

Kidd had to twist his body around like a pretzel while shooting the ball.

Next up for California were Hurley and the Blue Devils. The game was billed as the NCAA's best point guard against the next great college point guard. (The point guard on a basketball team is like the quarterback on a football team. The point guard calls the plays, makes the passes, and keeps the offense running the way it should.) The master, Hurley, would meet the student, Kidd. Not many people gave the Golden Bears much of a chance.

"California doesn't have a prayer against Duke," said a disgusted LSU coach Dale Brown after losing on Kidd's "pretzel" shot.

The level of excitement was high as the opening tip got the game under way. Kidd showed his stuff immediately by throwing a great alley-oop pass to forward Lamond Murray, who slammed the ball down for the game's first two points. The six-feet four-inch, 205-pound Kidd drove to the basket and threw terrific passes, to give the Golden Bears a ten-point lead at the half. The lead later grew to eighteen points, with eighteen minutes left in the contest.

It was clear that Bobby Hurley was not ready to give up his title as college basketball's best point guard. He nailed a bunch of three-point baskets and led Duke back to take a 77–76 lead, with just over two minutes left in the game.

Jason brought the ball upcourt and dribbled down to the low post. He drove along the left baseline but found his path blocked by a tight Blue Devils defense. He spotted Murray in the right corner and tried to get a pass to him. Hurley jumped up and made a great defensive play to deflect the ball, but suddenly the ball ended up back in Kidd's hands. Kidd threw up a prayer shot, and the ball went right in for what would be the game-winning basket.

Jason Kidd is able to score with circus-like shots when it is necessary. Perhaps his most famous is the "pretzel" shot that helped California to defeat LSU.

Kidd has a tremendous amount of speed, which allows him to weave through opposing defenses.

"I just followed my pass," Kidd later said, explaining how the ball ended up back in his hands. "Then I just threw it up there, like Joe Montana. I guess it was kind of a turnaround, hook shot." Joe Montana was a great football quarterback who was known for his incredible comebacks and acrobatic passes.

The Golden Bears held on to win the game, 82–77. Duke's championship run was over. Although Hurley outscored Kidd, the torch had clearly been passed. Jason Kidd was something special.

Chapter 2

Jason Frederick Kidd was born on March 23, 1973, in San Francisco, California.

"I was different from the day I was born," Kidd said. "Dad is black and Mom is white."

Jason's unusual background helped him experience and appreciate the two different cultures. His mother, Anne, is an Irish Catholic from San Francisco, while his father, Steve, is a Baptist from Missouri. His mom worked as a bank bookkeeper, and his dad was an airport ramp worker. Jason has two younger sisters, Denise and Kimberly.

"I had two different cultures and two different backgrounds to learn from," Kidd said. "I think that helped me to be special."

As a child, Jason dreamed of being a cowboy when he grew up. He liked the great western actor John Wayne. He would try to watch every western that came on television.

Jason was also very outgoing as a child. His middle-class family owned three horses. One day, Jason went on what his father thought would be a nice easy ride on an Appaloosa

Flying through the air, Kidd looks to pass off to an open teammate. As a child, Kidd learned to become a great passer by playing with kids much older than himself.

named Suki. Jason had other ideas. He decided to take the horse on a full gallop. His father was angry. He was afraid that Jason would get hurt.

"I wanted to get the gallop going the way that John Wayne did in the movies," Jason said. "But my father told me that I wasn't ready to go off at full speed right away. I was never too interested in riding after that."

As he got a little older, Jason traded in his cowboy hat for sporting equipment. He soon developed a love for sports. Jason was very good in many sports. He enjoyed playing football, baseball, soccer, and basketball. He was usually the youngest one on the basketball court, so he learned how to pass the ball to his older friends. Soon everyone wanted Jason on his or her team. It meant more shots for them.

"I was always one of the youngest ones, and for a long time I would be one of the last ones chosen to play," Jason said of his schoolyard pickup games. "So I learned how to pass. I figured the bigger kids would want me on their team if they knew I was more interested in getting them the ball and their shots in than in putting the ball up myself."

As Jason got older, his weekends were filled with playing sports. There would be soccer practice early in the morning, then baseball practice in the late afternoon. In between, Jason would spend all of his free time playing basketball with his friends or shooting baskets alone. He also liked to play football.

Jason attended a Catholic grammar school and was able to make the fourth-grade basketball team while he was still only in third grade. The coaches saw what a good athlete Jason was.

Although most of his formal sports training was in soccer, it was obvious from the start that Jason was going to be a very good basketball player. Jason developed a court sense and a

Dribbling into the key, Jason Kidd takes on two of the New Jersey Nets defenders.

knowledge of what the game was really about. It was not long before he started dominating games. He broke his first record in a fourth-grade game when he scored 21 of the team's 30 points.

Jason developed an aggressive, no-fear style that he brought to whatever sport he was playing. There was no better example of this than what he did during a Thanksgiving Day street football game when he was in the sixth grade. Jason caught a pass, knocked over a mailbox, and just kept going. He thought that he had broken his jaw.

That was the end of Jason's football career. His father put a stop to it. "I felt Jason would hurt himself because he's so aggressive," his father said.

Aggression and speed, two of Jason Kidd's traits, are perfect ingredients for the basketball court. Throw into the mix his rare gift of court vision, and you have the makings of a great basketball player. (Court vision is the ability to see everything on the basketball court. It is the strange knack of knowing when a defender is sneaking up on you from behind. It is the ability to predict when a teammate will break for the basket or flash from the low post. It is the ability to tell when a defender will back off or jump into a passing lane.) Court vision turned Earvin "Magic" Johnson into the greatest point guard ever to play the game. It would be the very thing that would carry Jason Kidd from fourth-grade superstar to college All-American to NBA superstar.

Chapter 3

By the time Jason was in the eighth grade, people began taking notice of what a natural he was on the basketball court.

"Everybody started saying how great Jason was," said his father, Steve Kidd. "We were flattered, but afraid to accept it. I guess by high school we started believing that he might be something special." Call that the understatement of the year.

Even before Jason finished grammar school, he was receiving letters from college coaches who were interested in him. While he was still just in the eighth grade, he would sometimes spend up to an hour after a game signing autographs.

"But he never got the big head," said his sister Denise. "He never acted like a superstar."

Kidd attended tiny St. Joseph's of Notre Dame High School, near Oakland. There he became an instant star. He impressed fans and teammates with his smart and flashy passing and his incredible leaping and twisting ability. It was also amazing how easily he embarrassed his defenders.

He led St. Joseph's to consecutive Division I state

championships in 1991 and 1992. Even more amazing was that St. Joseph's won 122 of the 136 games during Jason's four-year career. That was a winning percentage of .897! Jason became so popular that the team was forced to move some of its home games from its eight-hundred-seat gymnasium to the Oakland Coliseum. This was amazing because the school's enrollment was only around six hundred students.

"When I took Jason out during a lopsided game in front of 5,000 fans, I'll bet that 4,900 of them walked out," said Jason's high school coach, Frank LaPorte.

LaPorte was able to raise money for the school's athletic program because of Kidd. The school sold Jason Kidd basketball caps, T-shirts, and posters. At auctions, LaPorte had Jason sign basketballs. An autographed ball once sold for $750.

Jason's popularity soon became state—and nationwide. A reporter for the *Oakland Tribune* wrote in March 1992 that Kidd "is probably the most canonized, publicized, and analyzed prep school star in state history."

He was named the California Player of the Year during his junior and senior years. As a senior, he won the Naismith Award, which is given to the country's best high school player.

But the popularity was something that Jason did not like and was not ready for. He loved the attention on the court, he even thrived on the pressure, but he was uncomfortable when the spotlight was on him away from the court.

His parents tried to slow down the attention and media hype surrounding Jason, but there was not much they could do. They tried to limit his visits with the media and interviews to only after the games. After all, he still had to think about his studies.

By the time he was a senior, Jason had narrowed his list of

Kidd takes time out to sign autographs for basketball fans young and old. To raise money for his high school, Kidd would sign basketballs that would be sold at auctions.

potential colleges to Arizona, Kentucky, Kansas, and Ohio State. There was such competition for him that it seemed as if college coaches and recruiters were camping out on his front lawn. The only thing left to wait for was his score on the Scholastic Aptitude Test (SAT). He would have to score high enough to accept a basketball scholarship to one of these basketball powerhouses. Of course, there was also a rumor that Jason would skip college altogether and go directly to the National Basketball Association (NBA).

Jason did not do well on the test. He was very upset when this private matter was splattered all over the California newspapers. He took the test again, but the results were no better.

Jason became bitter about all the attention given to his off-the-court life, and he had some angry words for the media: "I know there are people out there who want to see me fail," he said. "They're laughing now but I will have the last laugh."

Jason's parents had taught him the value of hard work and patience. His father taught him that hard work would always pay off.

"When I was a kid, my father used to take me bowling," Kidd said. "I wasn't very good but I was always making excuses why I wasn't any good. My father said: 'Quit that. The reason you're not a good bowler is you don't practice.' And he was right. Now, if I have a defect, I work at it. I don't make any excuses."

Jason worked hard at improving his SAT scores and finally raised them enough to qualify for college. When he graduated from St. Joseph's in 1992, he announced that he wanted to attend a college far away from home. Most students know which college they will attend before their high school graduation. Some schools will hold one athletic scholarship open, hoping to lure an undecided athlete.

Jason shocked everyone when he announced that he was staying home. He had accepted an offer to play basketball at the University of California, in nearby Berkeley. "I want to be near my family and friends," he said of his decision to stay local.

Jason was familiar with the gymnasium and the campus after playing a lot of pickup games there. One of the other main reasons that he decided to attend UC Berkeley was that Golden Bears coach Lou Campanelli convinced his parents that the basketball program would stress studies and good grades. Jason was an average student who sometimes struggled to pass his classes. Campanelli, like many other college coaches, had followed Jason's career since Jason was in the eighth grade.

The hard part was seemingly over. Jason had escaped the microscope that he was forced to play under throughout grammar and high school. Now he was off to college and what looked to be a promising basketball career. The experts agreed that Jason was on the road to basketball stardom.

"He's in a class with the elite," said San Jose State coach Stan Morrison. "As a passer, he's right up there with Magic [Johnson] and [Bob] Cousy. The only thing is, he's a better athlete. He's got this explosive first step. As a passer he makes everybody so much better."

The fans were happy that Jason had decided to attend the University of California. The Golden Bears ticket office was swamped with five hundred phone calls the day Jason made his announcement.

The Golden Bears took a cue from St. Joseph's High School and moved five of their home games from the 6,578-seat Harmon Arena on campus to the Oakland Coliseum, which holds 15,000. The team drew impressive crowds. Jason performed well, but the team, which was 10–18 the year before he arrived, struggled. Coach Campanelli was fired halfway through the season. University officials wanted to hire a coach with a different attitude. Campanelli had a very hard, disciplined style that many of the players were not accustomed to.

Once again, the spotlight was on Jason. There were rumors that he was an influence in getting the coach fired. Jason's parents set the record straight. "My wife and I thought Campanelli was the greatest guy in the world," Jason's father said after hearing the accusations. "Jason never said anything like that to me."

Campanelli was replaced by assistant coach Todd Bozeman, who had spent a lot of time recruiting Jason for the school. He had a more relaxed style. He gave Jason full control of the offense, and told him to "take control." Bozeman wanted the Golden Bears to run more, and to try to score off the fast break. After all, he had one of the best point guards in the country. It was clear that California was at its best with Jason Kidd taking charge of the transition game. (In the transition period, the opposing team is setting up its defense. A good transition game results in easy baskets. It means pushing the basketball quickly up the court after grabbing a defensive rebound. A team needs a good and fast point guard to be a good transition team.)

Kidd clearly flourished under Bozeman and took his game to another level. He averaged 13.0 points, 7.7 assists, and 4.9 rebounds per game, to lead the Golden Bears to a 21–9 overall record, a 12–6 record in the highly competitive Pacific-10 Conference (Pac-10), and an NCAA tournament berth. Kidd's no-look passes, his confidence to attempt thread-the-needle passes, and his hard work ethic convinced people that he would be another Magic Johnson. He soon had his own following.

"Jason is a true student of the game," said Bozeman. "He

After a long recruiting war, Jason Kidd decided to play college basketball for the University of California. Kidd inspired teammates and fans with his excellent work ethic.

watches game film, studies his opponents' tendencies, breaks down other team's plays. He's able to see the game differently than most."

Kidd led the Bears to improbable victories against LSU and defending champion Duke during the NCAA tournament, bringing California into the elite Sweet Sixteen; the sixteen teams left playing in the tournament in the round before the quarterfinals. Kansas eliminated California, 93–76.

Jason Kidd and the Golden Bears accomplished much during his first season. He led California to its first national ranking in over thirty years. He was chosen National Freshman of the Year by *The Sporting News* after leading the Pac-10 with 222 assists and 110 steals. The only blemish on an otherwise great season for Kidd was his outside shooting. Although he averaged 13 points, he shot just 28.6 percent from three-point range.

Kidd spent the first few weeks of the summer touring Europe with Team USA, where he concentrated on improving his outside shooting. "I was just trying to be consistent and trying to shoot the ball the same way every time," he said. "I know my shot needs work, but I also know that when we need a big bucket, I want the shot—and I usually make it."

Just ask LSU and Duke.

The other thing Kidd did between his freshman and sophomore seasons at California was something that he had not done since grammar school: rest. Kidd, who had not taken more than three consecutive days off since grade school, took almost an entire month off from playing basketball. He felt that it would benefit him and his Golden Bear teammates.

"I feel a lot stronger," he said. "I'm well rested and mentally rested for a long season . . . an even longer season."

Kidd's goal was to take California to the Final Four.

Chapter 4

Just a few games into Kidd's second year at California, it became apparent that it would probably be his last season of college basketball. He was already one of the top five college players in the country, and the NBA was waiting.

Before the season started, the NCAA Rules Committee made some changes in the rules that gave the sophomore point guard even more of an advantage.

They reduced the shot clock from 45 seconds to 35 and eliminated the rule that dribblers had to give up the ball within five seconds of being guarded. This meant that a team had to attempt a shot at the basket within 35 seconds of getting the ball. In the NBA, teams have only 24 seconds to shoot.

Some experts believed the change was tailor-made for Kidd's game, but he took it all in stride. "I didn't think California really had a problem with the shot clock last year at 45 seconds," he said, "and I don't think we'll have a problem with it this year."

College basketball television analyst Billy Packer thought the change would drastically help Kidd. "This benefits Jason

Kidd's ball-handling skills are superb. Here he is shown shielding the ball from a defender.

for a couple of reasons," he said. "Number one, he's an excellent penetrator, a sensational passer . . . as good an open court passer as has been in the college game in quite some time."

Kidd came back for his second college season in better shape than ever. He had added ten pounds and worked out with weights. He was now a more muscular player.

Jason Kidd did not disappoint. He led the entire nation with 9.1 assists per game. He was also selected first-team All-American by *The Sporting News,* the Associated Press, and the U.S. Basketball Writers. He also set the Pac-10 single-season assist record with 272, and broke the single-game record with 18 assists. His scoring improved too. Jason averaged 16.7 points and 3.1 steals per game. The coaches in his conference named him the Pac-10 Player of the Year.

With 22 victories, California finished with better than twenty victories for the second straight season, earning them an invitation to the NCAA tournament. Although Kidd remained officially uncommitted about his basketball plans, everyone seemed to know that he would go professional after the season.

His mind was made up after highly ranked California lost in a shocking upset to the University of Wisconsin-Green Bay in the first round of the tournament. Kidd had a miserable game, connecting on only four of his seventeen shot attempts. He would forgo his last two years of college eligibility and enter the NBA draft. Kidd felt that he was ready for the NBA, and that he had taken this California team as far as it could go.

It helped Kidd's confidence that he played a lot of basketball, during his free time, with NBA players Gary Payton and Brian Shaw. "He's been destined for the NBA since he could walk," said Payton, an NBA All-Star.

Jason Kidd had a phenomenal sophomore season for California. He led the nation by dishing out 9.1 assists per game and was selected to the All-American team.

Kidd was proving his maturity on the basketball court. It was quite obvious that he was ready for the NBA. Then, his squeaky clean, All-American image became tarnished that spring after a few unfortunate incidents.

On May 22, 1994, Jason Kidd fled the scene of an accident. He later admitted he was the driver of a car that hit another and then overturned near an exit ramp on an Oakland highway.

"I was cruising about 65 miles per hour," Kidd later explained, "when something hit my car that caused me to go out of control." Kidd claimed that he was driving home two of his friends who had had too much to drink.

Kidd pleaded "no contest" to the misdemeanor charge of hit and run. He was given a fine and ordered to do a hundred hours of community service.

A few months earlier, on March 23, Jason Kidd threw a big birthday bash to celebrate his twenty-first birthday and his decision to turn professional. One of the people at his party claimed that Kidd hit her and pushed her. She filed criminal charges and then a lawsuit for $250,000.

Kidd denied that this happened. He felt the incident was an attempt to extort money from a soon-to-be-rich basketball player. The Alameda County District Attorney's office apparently agreed, and dismissed all charges.

"That was definitely a money incident," Kidd later said. "It is something that happens to every player in their career. With me, somehow it happened before my career got started."

On top of all this, Kidd fathered a child out of wedlock. He was ordered by the courts to pay child support.

These three incidents made NBA officials very nervous about drafting Kidd. Many teams ask players to undergo psychiatric tests and a background check into their character before taking a gamble and drafting them. It was a foregone conclusion that Kidd was one of the best basketball players to come around in a long time, but he needed to show that he was responsible and mature as well.

"Jason has a lot of energy. A lot," said his mother, Anne. "You've got to keep Jason busy and occupied. You must, or he gets himself into trouble."

There was plenty of debate around Kidd as the NBA draft grew closer. "Court vision," said Sam Schuler, the San Antonio Spurs personnel director. "He's got unbelievable court vision."

Donnie Walsh, president of the Indiana Pacers, agreed. "His strength and speed alone will help make an immediate impact."

The Dallas Mavericks owned the second pick of the draft and were leaning heavily toward taking Kidd. Dallas was in sore need of a young, talented point guard to run its offense. The Mavs already had two tremendously talented scorers in forward Jamal Mashburn and off-guard or shooting guard Jimmy Jackson.

Dallas coach Dick Motta met with Kidd and asked him very candid questions about the incidents. He did not want to draft "damaged goods." "It's our job to find out if it's a tip-of-an-iceberg sign or not," Motta said. "I've been burned in my career. I'll be darned if I'm not going to treat this seriously."

Kidd was very confident. He wanted to prove his critics wrong. "Hopefully, the good things said about me will be true, about changing the league and adding a lot to it," he said. Regarding the events of 1994, he said, "those incidents were isolated. Everybody has an opinion. Some feel that I will be a flop. But if [the Mavericks] win a world championship with me, I'd like to see what those same people will have to say. I'm ready to play in the NBA."

Walsh agreed with the character investigations but also

believed that Kidd would be just fine. "A few years ago, everyone was saying that Reggie Miller was the worst kid that ever lived. I don't know where it came from, but after we brought him out [to Indiana], we knew right away nothing was true. I can't see it affecting Jason that much."

Reggie Miller has been one of the best scorers in the NBA since he came into the league in 1987.

Many believed that leaving the Bay area and going into the draft early would benefit Kidd greatly. He was larger than life, a superstar before he was even in high school. There was a tremendous amount of pressure on Kidd in his hometown. He needed to get away from that pressure and from some friends who may not have been good influences on him.

After going through workouts and interviews, Kidd convinced most teams that he would be a good draft pick.

"He's just tailor-made for the NBA," Schuler said. "Court vision and great hands, especially at the defensive end are hard to overlook. He has all the qualities, tangible and intangibles, that you want in a point guard."

The Dallas Mavericks were convinced, and they chose Kidd with the second pick of the 1994 NBA draft. He was drafted behind Glenn Robinson of Purdue and ahead of Duke's Grant Hill.

Kidd was glad to be drafted so high and to be joining one of the youngest teams in the league. "It's going to be exciting to be passing to Jimmy [Jackson], Jamal [Mashburn], Sean Rooks," he said at the draft. "My idol is Magic Johnson and only Magic. I've looked up to him and tried to follow in his footsteps. I know that's a hard thing to do, but I really patterned my game after Magic."

Johnson had words of praise for Kidd as well. "I love his attitude," Johnson said. "He'll make a great pass that finds a teammate free for a dunk, then he hustles back to play defense. I love it."

The Dallas Mavericks chose Jason Kidd with the second pick in the 1994 NBA draft. Among his new teammates were Jimmy Jackson (far left), considered to be an exciting young scorer, and George McCloud, a three-point specialist.

The Mavericks, eager to turn things around after having several losing seasons in a row, decided to lock up their new talented point guard with a long-term contract. The Mavs signed Kidd to a nine-year contract worth about $60 million.

Jason Kidd, the boy wonder who had dazzled fans in grammar school, high school, and college, was now ready to live out his dream. He was now in the NBA.

Chapter 5

At only twenty-one years of age, Jason Kidd was already a multimillionaire and the starting point guard for an NBA team. As he entered training camp for his first professional season, he tried to put to rest the lingering questions regarding his character. "I've got to develop a strategy to deal with this," he said. "I've got to find out how to be the real Jason Kidd."

Dallas was the perfect situation for him. The Mavericks were already loaded up with plenty of players who could score. They needed a leader. Kidd could take time to work on his offensive game, especially his outside shooting, which remained the only weak part of his game. The Mavs did not need him to score a lot of points. Dallas was also perfect for Kidd because the team had hired veteran coach Dick Motta to be the new head coach. Motta, well respected and well liked around the league, was able to offer Kidd the right amount of patience and nurturing that his game needed.

"If we work hard and listen to Coach Motta," Kidd said, "then we will be successful."

Kidd's hard work impressed his teammates and coach

right from the start of training camp. He learned the team's entire playbook in one day. Not only did he learn what was expected of the point guard on every play, but he also memorized where the other four players should be on every play.

He still knew that there was much more to be done. "I have a lot to learn about the game of basketball," he said. "Right now, I'm just being a sponge and trying to absorb it all."

Right from the start, it was plain to see that the Dallas Mavericks with Jason Kidd running the offense were a far cry from the Mavs of the previous two seasons. Dallas was a terrible 11–71 for the 1992–93 season and only 13–69 in 1993–94. With Kidd at the point, the Mavs jumped out to an 11–8 start, already equalling their victory total of two seasons ago.

Kidd was intense on defense. He showed incredible speed with and without the ball. His flying blocks of an opponent's shot, and his spectacular no-look bounce passes, gained him a fast reputation around the league.

"I just love to watch him play," said his teammate Mashburn after only a few games.

Early in Kidd's rookie season, the Mavs stunned their cross-state rivals, the San Antonio Spurs. After the game, Spurs coach Bob Hill paid Kidd a special compliment: "He's a man. He manhandled us. His stats don't mean a thing. He's a special player. He played like a veteran," he said.

Kidd did a lot of things during that game that helped result in an overtime victory for Dallas. The beauty and effectiveness of his play are not usually seen in statistics or in box scores. He gives the extra effort and usually hustles and dives after loose balls. He protects the ball on offense and hounds the ball on defense. More important, he uses a

An intense defensive player, Jason Kidd tries to make sure Robert Pack has nowhere to go.

combination of instincts and thinking on the floor. Court vision!

Kidd was impressing everyone, even legends. "I don't say this about a lot of NBA players today," said Hall of Fame point guard Bob Cousy, "but I'd pay to see Kidd play."

Another example of Kidd's explosive play was displayed during a game against the Los Angeles Lakers. He hurt his elbow early in the game and was unable to return to the floor until midway through the second quarter. The Mavs were down by nine points. In exactly one minute and twenty seconds, Kidd was able to turn the game around.

With 9:30 left in the quarter, Kidd drove down the court for an easy layup. Then he slipped a no-look pass to center Roy Tarpley, who dunked. Then Kidd stole the ball and found teammate Lucious Harris for another dunk. Kidd then hustled back on defense and was able to break up a two-on-one fast break without committing a foul. He found Tarpley again for another dunk. After a few foul shots, the Mavs had taken a one-point lead, with 8:10 left in the quarter.

The Lakers ended up winning the game, 113–108, in part because Kidd missed several short jump shots throughout the game. He had been shooting a miserable 30 percent from the field until then.

Kidd has perfect mechanics when he shoots the ball, except at the very end. He releases the ball a little too quickly. It is something he knows about and works on every day. "I have to be patient," he said. "I know my jump shooting will come around. I've been shooting very well in practice. But I have to see what others have gone through, like Gary Payton."

Payton, the All-Star point guard of the Seattle SuperSonics, gradually improved his offensive skills to become one of the outstanding point guards and scorers in the game. "When Gary came up he didn't shoot with much

Coming into the league, Kidd knew that his shooting was not the strongest part of his game. Therefore, he continues to practice his shot to make himself better.

confidence," Kidd said, "but now he'll score 35 or 40 points in a game."

Poor shooting aside, Kidd starred in just about every other category, from steals to assists to turnovers. He also proved to be one of the game's best rebounding guards. But what put Kidd on the path to stardom was his hard play. Kidd is pure energy on the basketball court. He is usually so exhausted and so full of aches and pains after a basketball game that he can hardly stand. He plays with such enthusiasm and fire that he often has to sit on a stool while he takes his shower after a game. It was a running joke in the Mavericks' locker room that Kidd sat on his throne while he took a bath.

Besides sitting in the shower, Kidd has another locker room tradition in his routine. He keeps a Ken Griffey, Jr., rookie baseball card in his locker for good luck. "Junior is the best in baseball," he says. "My goal is to be the best in basketball."

Kidd helped lead the Mavericks to a respectable 34–46 season, a whopping twenty-three-game improvement over the previous year. Kidd averaged 11.7 points per game, 7.7 assists, 5.4 rebounds, and 1.91 steals per game. He ranked seventh in the league in steals and ninth in assists.

Kidd was named NBA Player of the Week for the third week in March 1995 and was named the Rookie of the Month for March. He also led the league in triple-doubles with four. (A triple-double occurs when a player records ten or more in three of these four categories—points, assists, rebounds, or blocks—in a single game.)

After the season, it was announced that Kidd, along with Detroit rookie superstar Grant Hill, had been named cowinners of the Rookie of the Year award. Each player received 43 of a possible 105 votes, to finish in a tie. It was the first tie in twenty-four years for Rookie of the Year. The award was a great honor for Kidd and vindication against those who doubted him.

Kidd did some good things off the court that year as well. One of the best things he did was to give $46,000 to a church in Dallas to help build a gymnasium. The gym would be used to start a youth basketball league in the area. "In this day and age," he said, "kids need a place to go."

Kidd bought thirty tickets for every Dallas home game to give to underprivileged children. He also began donating a few thousand dollars to his old high school every year.

Just before his second professional season started, there was a local debate in the newspapers about whether the Mavericks had made the right choice in picking Jason Kidd ahead of Grant Hill in the draft. A few games into the season, Kidd had squashed the debate. While Hill is a tremendous player and scorer, there is no denying that it is much more valuable to have a great point guard to run the offense.

Barely two weeks into his sophomore campaign, Kidd was already crossing the line from outstanding player to superstar.

In the season opener at San Antonio, Kidd showed everyone his offensive game by hitting 11 of 17 buckets and scoring 27 points. He also dominated passing, defense, and rebounding. The next night, in the Mavs' home opener, Kidd kept himself out of the offensive spotlight as he sensed that some of his teammates had the hot shooting touch. He made only two of five baskets but once again dominated the opposing point guard, as Dallas won its first two.

Kidd tried to explain the word "superstar" as Dallas climbed to a 4–0 start. "For some, the word superstar is a strong description, but it's been in my dictionary for a long time," he said. "Going back to Junior High, people have wanted to tag me with that. Some players thrive on it but

Moving with the ball, Jason Kidd tries to spot the open man.

others don't want that kind of pressure. But me, I think I'm indifferent. It doesn't bother me, except there's a tendency in sports to separate that description from team player. Being a team player is something I've always strived for, something I take the most pride in. It would really bother me a lot if anyone ever thought I sacrificed being a team player in order to achieve an individual reputation like that."

In a league of great point guards, past and present, Jason Kidd was quickly proving that he belonged right there with the best of them.

Chapter 6

By midseason it was obvious that being a superstar was not the final stop in Kidd's young career. As he moved his way up the ladder, he seemed likely to join the NBA's legendary players.

In his second season, Kidd was voted the starting point guard for the Western Conference All-Star Team. He became the first player in Mavericks history to start an All-Star game. In Dallas's last game before the All-Star Game, Kidd played a great game, with an unbelievable 25-assist night, against one of the all-time great point guards, all-time assist leader, John Stockton. Kidd showed why he belonged on the All-Star team.

Kidd shied away from the attention, saying that he was "just in a zone passing the ball, that's all." Not wanting to upstage such a great point guard, he said that he would be happy to carry Stockton's water if the two were on the same team.

For Kidd, making the All-Star team was yet another dream come true. "I used to sit in front of the television and just envision what it would be like," he said.

Eric Montross congratulates Jason Kidd on making a fine play. In 1996, basketball fans showed their appreciation for Kidd by selecting him as the starting point guard for the Western Conference All-Star Team.

During the last couple of years, the All-Star game has become a slam-dunking, three-point shooting free-for-all that the average fan enjoys just fine. But, for the true fan of the sport, a lot of the fun is in watching the point guard create and execute a beautiful pass.

"Basketball is about making the pass, about finding a means to connect moving dots," noted *The New York Times* basketball writer Harvey Araton. "Most everything else, with the obvious exception of Michael Jordan, had the potential to become repetitiously banal. The smart and well-executed pass, fortunately never gets old."

Kidd filled up an entire reel of highlights during a six-minute stretch in the first quarter. He put on an incredible passing show filled with no-looks, lobs, and lead passes. He had the San Antonio audience gasping and cheering. Western coach George Karl, of the Seattle SuperSonics, was obligated to play all three of his point guards, so Kidd finished the game having played only twenty-two minutes. But he stole the show with his incredible six-minute run. He scored 7 points, had 10 assists, and added 6 rebounds.

"Jason Kidd is going to be basketball's most electric innovator for some time," Araton wrote after the game.

Western Conference teammate and future basketball Hall-of-Famer Charles Barkley was equally impressed. "Playing with this guy [Jason], it's like it is with Magic," he said. "You have to be looking at him every second."

The Eastern Conference went on to win the game, 129–118. Anyone who had not heard of Jason Kidd before the game was sure to have heard of him now.

Kidd was equally impressed. "I grew up watching Larry Bird, Isiah Thomas and Magic [Johnson] battle, the East against the West, it was always a thrill," he said. "Now that I have experienced it, I look forward to many more. And hopefully I can start a lot more."

Kidd also viewed playing in his first All-Star game as a learning experience. "It was great playing in the All-Star game," he continued. "It helped me gain a lot of confidence and that's all I really need. I want to continue to gain confidence because I think that it will not only help me on the court, but off the court too. There was no pressure for me to do this or that. I just went out and played my game."

Kidd realized however, that in order to become a superstar, he would have to continue to work hard. "I'm not going to let all this All-Star stuff go to my head," he said. "I'm only as good as my last game. However I did like playing in the All-Star game. And being known as one of the twenty-four best players for that one weekend, was a great experience. I will always remember it."

Unfortunately for Kidd, the All-Star game would be the high point of his season. Although he continued to play great basketball, the Dallas Mavericks were suffering through a terrible season. They lost small forward and outstanding scorer Jamal Mashburn to knee surgery early in the season. The team fell on especially hard times in March when it dropped 14 out of 17 games, including an 11-game losing streak. The Mavs also lost veteran center Roy Tarpley to substance abuse and were left without any inside game at all. Because of that, the Mavs often resorted to shooting three-pointers as their offense. They wound up setting single-game and season records for three-pointers attempted and made. But that is not how playoff-caliber teams execute.

Still, Kidd played exceptionally well, impressing everyone who saw him. "Jason Kidd is something special," said Coach Motta. "He's one of those players who makes everyone else around him a little better. He's the best I've ever had and I've had a bunch of good ones."

The Dallas bench appears to be disgusted by what they see. Injuries and personal problems caused the 1995–96 season to be extremely disappointing for Dallas.

Even opposing players began paying tribute to Kidd. "I have all the respect in the world for him and I think it is mutual," said point guard Derek Harper, who used to play for Dallas but was now running the point for the New York Knicks. "Jason is very good, very competitive. The sky's the limit for him. He's going to be a great point guard."

The losing began to take its toll on Kidd. He was used to winning consistently on every level, from grammar school through college. "I'm not used to this," he said. "I'm not used to losing the way that we have been losing. I don't want to hurt anyone's feelings or anything like that, but we're a pretty good team when you take away all the negative things."

In addition to Mashburn's injury and Tarpley's suspension, Kidd was talking about a feud between him and a teammate, Jimmy Jackson. It got so bad at one point that he asked the team to trade either him or Jackson away. The club denied his request, and the players tried to work out their differences.

Kidd finished his second season with 9 triple doubles, second in the NBA to Grant Hill's 10. He also had a club record 783 assists, along with 553 rebounds. He became only the sixth player in NBA history to top 700 assists and 500 rebounds in the same season.

He finished second in the league in assists, averaging 9.7 a game, and fourth in steals, averaging more than two a game. Kidd was even named NBA Player of the Week for the week of January 29 to February 4. One of his biggest improvements was in his scoring average. It improved from 11.7 points per game as a rookie to 16.6 points per game in his second season.

"Jason is one of those throwbacks," said NBA head coach Chuck Daly. "I liken him to players that we've known in the past, like Bob Cousy, who love to pass. He's one of those people that you love to watch play. He doesn't have to score a

Jimmy Jackson and Jason Kidd listen to what teammate Eric Montross has to say. Another problem that plagued the Mavericks was a dispute between Kidd and Jackson.

point to be brilliant, and really has made a mark in the game. He is going to continue to be better as his scoring improves."

The Mavericks finished with a terrible 26–56 record and a sixth-place finish in the Midwest Division. But a healthy Jamal Mashburn and a bona fide center to go along with one of the best point guards in the game would surely help turn things around.

Chapter 7

The disappointing season for the Dallas Mavericks hit even more of a low when team owner Donald Carter, Dallas's only owner in its sixteen years of existence, decided to sell the team. But it also provided a good example of Kidd's importance.

The prospective buyers, a group led by Ross Perot Jr., the son of Texas billionaire and two-time presidential nominee Ross Perot, wanted to speak with Kidd before and after buying the team. They were interested in his input regarding personnel decisions. It is very rare that a team owner wants to speak directly with an athlete regarding a sale.

"Jason's input is very important to the sale of the club," Carter said. Carter decided to keep about 20 percent of the team. "I feel very excited about the future of this team, about maybe getting a new arena to play in, about everything."

Kidd expressed a strong desire to remain in Dallas and also hoped that the new owners would keep Motta as the head coach. "I think we need Coach Motta," he said. "I really hope he's the coach next year."

The new owners took his advice under consideration but

decided to go in a fresh and new direction. They hired Jim Cleamons, a former NBA guard and assistant coach of the defending champion Chicago Bulls, as their new head coach. One thing in particular that made Cleamons attractive was the fact that he owned four NBA championship rings. He knew how to win, and the new owners hoped he could teach his new young team the same. Then Dallas added a pair of proven and capable big bodies in Eric Montross and Oliver Miller, and it also added point guard insurance in signing free agent Derek Harper. Harper, known throughout the league for his toughness and his leadership abilities, was expected to add some much-needed harmony to the team as well as to help Kidd continue his learning process. He is also still one heck of a point guard.

The Mavericks still started the 1996–97 season without a bona fide intimidating center, but looked like a lock to improve on their 1995–96 record.

The Mavs suffered a scare in the preseason when Kidd strained his right knee during practice. Tests showed that there was damage, but he was ready to go by opening day, which was bad news for opposing NBA coaches.

"As far as a point guard, Jason Kidd has some of the greatest passing skills I have ever seen," said former point guard and Milwaukee Bucks head coach Mike Dunleavy. "I would put him in a class with Magic Johnson and John Stockton." Dunleavy is now Milwaukee's general manager.

No matter how much Kidd improves and leads his team, it seems that his critics always point to his shooting percentage. Even though he improved his scoring average nearly five points, he still shot only 38 percent from the field. With a healthy Mashburn and Jackson constantly being double-teamed, Kidd would continue to get his share of shots.

"With all the double-teams we see, I get plenty of wide

Prior to the 1996–97 season, the Mavericks added point guard Derek Harper to their team. A former Mavericks star, Harper was brought in to provide veteran leadership to the troubled Dallas team.

open looks," he said. "I have to shoot it. My coach and teammates are behind me and I know that sooner or later I'll get my rhythm down and my confidence up and they'll start going in."

Even if Kidd's shooting remained just mediocre, his incredible court vision and gift of passing the ball would put him in the record books and help lead the Mavericks for a long time to come. For a player who had an incredible second year in the NBA, Kidd said his biggest thrills of the season were watching Jackson and Mashburn record 50-point games. He is a true point guard: unselfish.

The city of Dallas is used to winning championships. After all, the Dallas Cowboys have appeared in more Super Bowls than any other team in football. While the Cowboys are fueled by three superstars—Troy Aikman, Emmitt Smith, and Michael Irvin—the Mavericks hoped that their three young budding superstars would translate into championships for their franchise. Jackson, Mashburn, and Kidd were being touted as the three J's. All three were extremely talented and had a world of potential.

But the 1996–97 season started badly. Kidd feuded often with the new coach, Jim Cleamons, about how the offense should run. Kidd preferred a faster running style, while Cleamons tried to run the Chicago Bulls' triple-post offense. The team played poorly, and on the day after Christmas the Mavericks shocked the NBA by trading Jason Kidd to the Phoenix Suns. Kidd was sent to the Suns, along with Tony Dumas and Loren Meyer, in exchange for Sam Cassell, Michael Finley, A. C. Green, and a second-round draft pick.

Former player and coach Don Nelson was hired as the general manager of the Mavericks later that season, and he quickly cleaned house. He traded Jimmy Jackson and Eric Montross to the New Jersey Nets, along with Sam Cassell,

Jason Kidd looks to feed an open teammate for an easy shot. Kidd gets his greatest thrills from helping his teammates have really big games.

Chris Gatling, and George McCloud, in exchange for Shawn Bradley, Robert Pack, Ed O'Bannon, and Khalid Reeves. Nelson also traded Mashburn to the Miami Heat for Sasha Danilovic, Kurt Thomas, and Martin Maursepp. The Mavericks would have to start all over again.

Meanwhile, Kidd brought his fiery brand of basketball to one of the worst teams in basketball: the Phoenix Suns.

Chapter 8

Jason Kidd has toyed with the idea of playing professional baseball in the off-season. He was one of the best players on his high school team, and he is sure that he could make the jump to the pros. Deion Sanders plays both professional football and baseball. Kidd's new coach with the Suns, Danny Ainge, was once a baseball player with the Toronto Blue Jays. Ainge went on to enjoy a fine basketball career with the Boston Celtics, Portland Trailblazers, and Sacramento Kings, as well as the Suns.

In college, Kidd would sometimes practice with the baseball team. "I would go out and take some batting practice with the fellas to show them I could have played baseball if I wanted, if I put in the time," he said.

Kidd also likes to play golf during his free time. Sometimes he plays golf with Michael Jordan. He also enjoys listening to rap music. Luckily for the Phoenix Suns, though, his first love is basketball.

To this day, Kidd is still very close to his family. His

father, Steve, often flies around the country to watch his games. He speaks with his mother a lot on the telephone.

The Suns began the 1996–97 season with a terrible start. They lost their first thirteen games of the season. Kidd broke his collarbone during his first game with the Suns and did not join them until February.

The time off was good for Kidd. He was very hurt that the Mavericks had traded him. The time spent waiting for his shoulder to heal helped him get over it. "I never thought they would trade me," he said after the deal. "I still can't believe it."

Ainge already had a very talented, but aging, point guard in Kevin Johnson, so many people wondered what Ainge would do when Kidd returned from his injury. That was simple. He played them both at the same time. He called it his two-point guard offense. Kidd played well, and the Suns became one of the hottest teams after the All-Star break.

Even though they started the season with thirteen straight losses, Kidd helped them make the playoffs. It would be his first time in postseason play.

Johnson especially enjoyed having Kidd around, as it seemed to revitalize his career. Johnson averaged better than twenty points and nine assists after Kidd joined the team. Kidd also enjoyed having another point guard on the floor with him.

There was not as much pressure to lead the team, and Kidd took the opportunity to score some points. On March 17, 1997, he tied a career high with 33 points on 12 for 16 shooting, including eight out of nine three-pointers. The Suns beat the Golden State Warriors, 116–95.

"For somebody who can't shoot the ball," Kidd said, laughing, "that's not bad."

Phoenix finished the season with a 40–42 record. This was

Jason Kidd was traded to the Phoenix Suns in the middle of the 1996–97 season. The Suns were in last place at the time of the trade, but Kidd helped lead them to the playoffs.

good enough to earn them the seventh spot in the Western Conference playoffs. Kidd and the Suns faced the Western Conference defending champs, the Seattle SuperSonics.

Phoenix went into the series as the underdog, but by using a very different four-guard offense, they stole the first game of the best of five series, 106–101.

Coach Ainge decided to use the four-guard offense to counter Seattle's superior size with the Suns' superior quickness. Johnson and Kidd ran the offense efficiently. Seattle evened the series in the second game, but then Phoenix took Game 3, 110–103.

After dropping Game 4 in overtime, the Suns looked to Johnson and Kidd to lead them to an improbable victory. They played their hearts out, but Seattle was just too much for them, winning 116–92.

Kidd scored 17 points, passed for 7 assists, and pulled down 8 rebounds in a losing effort. Johnson also added 20 points in defeat.

While Kidd enjoys being on the floor with Johnson, another great point guard, the Suns will be looking for Kidd to be the future of the team. Johnson has played for a long time and has had a lot of injuries. When Johnson decides to retire, Kidd will take over the team. Whatever the task, Jason Kidd, with his no-look passes and intense defense, will be ready.

Career Statistics

College

YEAR	TEAM	GP	FG%	REB	AST	PTS	AVG
1992–93	California	29	.463	142	222	378	13.0
1993–94	California	30	.472	207	272	500	16.7
Totals		59	.468	349	494	878	14.9

NBA

YEAR	TEAM	GP	FG%	REB	AST	STL	BLK	PTS	AVG
1994–95	Dallas	79	.385	430	607	151	24	922	11.7
1995–96	Dallas	81	.381	553	783	175	26	1,348	16.6
1996–97	Dallas/ Phoenix	55	.403	249	496	124	20	599	10.9
Totals		215	.387	1,232	1,886	450	70	2,869	13.3

GP=Games Played
FG%=Field Goal Percentage
REB=Rebounds

AST=Assists
STL=Steals
BLK=Blocks

PTS=Points
AVG=Points Per Game

Where to Write Jason Kidd:

Mr. Jason Kidd
c/o Phoenix Suns
P.O. Box 1369
Phoenix, AZ 85001

Index

L

LaPorte, Frank, 18
Los Angeles Lakers, 37
Louisiana State University, 7, 24

M

Mashburn, Jamal, 30–31, 46, 48, 50, 52, 54, 56
McCloud, George, 56
Meyer, Loren, 54
Miami Heat, 56
Miller, Oliver, 52
Miller, Reggie, 31
Milwaukee Bucks, 52
Montana, Joe, 11
Montross, Eric, 52, 54
Murray, Lamond, 8

N

Nelson, Don, 54
New Jersey Nets, 54
1996 NBA All-Star Game, 43, 46

O

Oakland Coliseum, 18, 21
Oakland Tribune, 18
O'Bannon, Ed, 56
Ohio State University, 20

P

Packer, Billy, 25, 27
Payton, Gary, 27, 37, 39

Perot, Ross, Jr., 51
Purdue University, 31

R

Reeves, Khalid, 56
Robinson, Glenn, 31
Rookie of the Year Award, 39
Rooks, Sean, 31

S

St. Joseph's of Notre Dame High School, 17–18, 20–21
San Antonio Spurs, 30, 35, 40
San Jose State University, 21
Sanders, Deion, 57
Schuler, Sam, 30, 31
Seattle SuperSonics, 37, 45, 60
Shaw, Brian, 27
Smith, Emmitt, 54
The Sporting News, 24, 27
Stockton, John, 43, 52

T

Tarpley, Roy, 37, 46, 48
Thomas, Isiah, 45

W

Walsh, Donnie, 30–31
Wayne, John, 12, 14
Wisconsin-Green Bay, University of, 27